Grimy, Grubby Gardening

Kentucky Kids dig it!

KAREN ANGELUCCI

Illustrations by James Asher

Copyright © 2009 by McClanahan Publishing House, Inc.

International Standard Book Number 978-1-934898-04-8
Library of Congress Card Catalog Number 2009929769

Cover design and book layout by Asher Graphics
Illustrations by James Asher

Manufactured in China

Sources:
United States Department of Agriculture
Kentucky Cooperative Extension Service
Arbor Day Foundation
www.americanforest.org
American Horticulture Society

All book order correspondence
should be addressed to:

McClanahan Publishing House, Inc.
P.O. Box 100
Kuttawa, KY 42055

270-388-9388
800-544-6959
270-388-6186 FAX

www.kybooks.com

For

Sarah and Rachel
My beautiful flowers

I could not have created this book without the
support of my husband, Mike, and my daughters,
Sarah and Rachel.

I would like to thank Dorotha Smith Oatts for
her unwavering support for more education. I also
need to thank my dear friends Barbara Mabry,
Yvette Hurt, Dave Leonard, Melissa Burton,
Sandy Young, Camille Bradley and Debbie Kiser
for their honest opinions.

And lastly, I thank my parents, Nelson and
Carolyn Williams, who let me rip and run through
the countryside of Cynthiana as a child. This
freedom allowed me to become the nature lover
I am today.

Karen Angelucci

Introduction

My love for gardening began at a very early age. I have always felt that you need to get dirty and up close and personal with nature in order to fully understand it. I hope you have an opportunity to plant a seed, water a plant, or pick a strawberry.

I wrote *Grimy Grubby Gardening* to help you learn to love the art of gardening and take that special gift with you throughout your life.

Serious Stuff

To make sure you have a safe gardening experience be sure to follow these instructions.

1 Always work with an adult.
2 Never eat plants unless an adult says it is safe. Some plants can make you very sick.
3 Be careful with gardening tools. Always lay tools with pointy side down.
4 Do not use chemicals. Use only fertilizer, compost, and manure that come from vegetables or animals.
5 Wash hands after gardening or, better yet, take a bath.

What do plants need?

Plants need the sun.

The sun provides warmth and light that gives energy to plants. The structure of plants above the ground includes **leaves**, **buds**, **stems**, flowers and/or fruits. Stems transport food and water and support the leaves. Leaves allow sunlight to be collected and absorbed. This process is called **photosynthesis**, and it changes carbon dioxide that the plants naturally breathe into sugar. This sugar is a form of food for the plants.

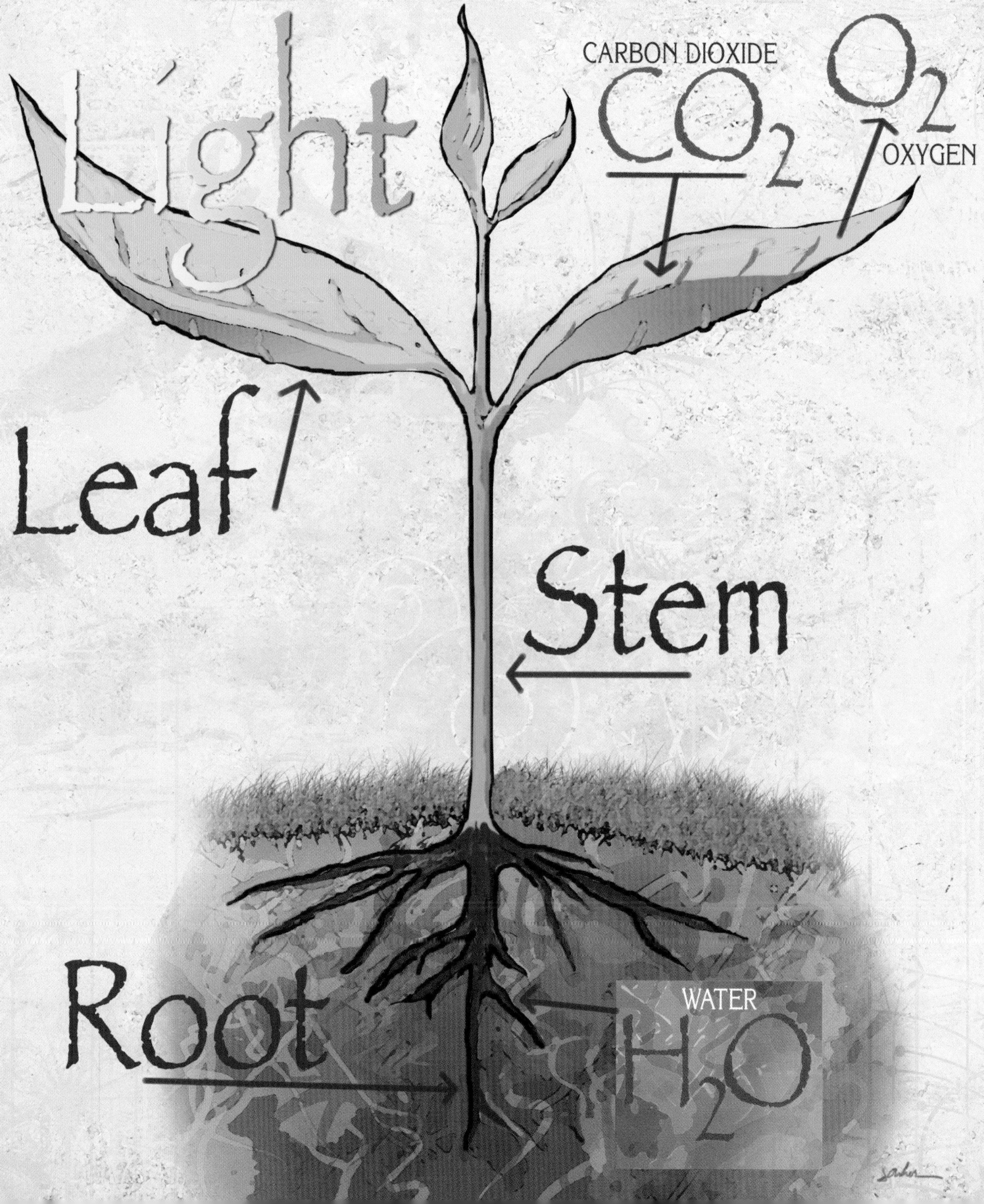
Light
CARBON DIOXIDE
CO_2
O_2
OXYGEN
Leaf
Stem
Root
WATER
H_2O

Plants need clean air.

Clean, fresh air is important to grow healthy plants and children. Plants breathe air through their leaves and **roots**. Plants clean the air by removing harmful gases, making the air cleaner for people and plants. Breezes strengthen stems and leaves by forcing their roots to grow stronger.

Plants need healthy roots and soil so they can grow big and strong.

1. Select a site that is good for what you want to grow. Most vegetables require full sun. Some flowers need shade. It is best to find a site close to a water source. Make your garden at least 4 by 6 feet. The site should also drain well. Remove grass, weeds, bits of trash, and break up large clumps of soil with a shovel.

2. Prepare soil by adding **fertilizer**, **compost**, and aged **manure**. This is called **organic** gardening.

3. Dig garden to about 12 inches deep with a shovel.

4. Use a metal rake to smooth the soil before planting and sowing.

5. Create shallow rows about 8 inches apart, or mounds in the soil, with a garden hoe. To keep the rows straight, tie a string to two stakes, one at each end, and place in the center of each row.

6. Plant **seeds** according to the instructions on the seed packet. Pay attention to how deep they should be planted and how far apart to plant each seed. Cover seeds lightly with soil.

7. Always soak well with water and keep soil moist (not wet) every day until seeds sprout.

8. After seeds sprout, you will need to make room by **thinning** or pulling up some **seedlings**. Try to keep plants 4 to 6 inches apart.

Roots are the underground portion of a plant. Roots are designed to anchor the plant, absorb minerals and water, and store food.

Soil holds air, water, minerals, **organic matter**, and anchors each plant so it can grow.

Soil is made up of three sizes of mineral particles: large particles are sand, medium particles are silt, and the smallest particles make up clay.

Have a parent or adult work with you while you prepare soil for planting.

Leaf Stem

Root

Kids, look for hidden treasures in the soil such as buttons, coins, paper clips, gems!

Plants need food.

Just as people need food, so do plants. Most plant food or nutrients are already in the soil. Improving the soil with fertilizer or compost will grow healthier plants.

Plant food comes in many forms such as liquid or granular. You can buy fertilizer at the store or you can make plant food in a compost bin. Liquid and granular fertilizer should be used as directed on the bottle, bag or can. Aged manure and compost can be scattered around the plants and worked into the soil.

Most plants will need to be fed on the first day you see sprouting stems and then every 4 weeks.

N-P-K defined:

(N) Nitrogen: increases leaf and stem growth, increases green color, quick energy, quick results. Spring is the best season for nitrogen application. Nitrogen is very soluble and dissolves from the soil quickly.

(P) Phosphorus: increases root development, fruit production, and seeds. Phosphorus is necessary for good plant health and has a major role in setting of flower and fruit. Phosphorus moves through the soil slowly.

(K) Potassium, also called potash: increases flowers and fruit, aids in cold and disease resistance. Potassium is soluble in water, but in clay soil it doesn't move quickly. Note: (K) is from Kalium, the Latin word for potassium.

Make a compost pile.

Composting is a way to recycle decomposing material to feed plants.

1   Find a partly sunny spot that is sheltered from strong winds and is near the garden and water hose. It is best to keep your compost pile away from doors and windows.

2   Build a square, or round, bin to hold compost or use any container with the bottom cut out. Place compost pile directly on the soil. This will create a habitat for worms, dragonflies, spiders, snails, slugs, beetles, and caterpillars.

3   Start with a 5-inch layer of chopped dry material, such as leaves or straw.

4   Next layer with wet material, such as weeds, green grass, or kitchen scraps (apple cores, coffee grounds, and egg shells).

5   The trick is to not let it get too wet or too dry. If it begins to stink then you know it is probably too wet. So add dry materials.

6   Every few weeks take a shovel, or pitch fork, and turn the pile. This allows air inside for the worms and insects that live there.

7   Always wear disposable gloves when working with compost and wash your hands when you are finished.

8   Be patient! This process takes six to eighteen months to break down. The pile will heat up and break down into rich, fertile food for your garden.

Do not put in your compost pile:
Invasive grasses and vines
Diseased or insect infested plants
Any plant treated with a chemical
Dairy products
Bread
Animal fats
Meat products
Pet manure
Oils
Waxes
Poisonous plants
Plastic

Pile it on!
Shredded leaves
Lawn clippings
Soil
Plant debris
Hay/straw
Tea and coffee grounds
Dust from vacuum bags
Spoiled cereals
Fruit and vegetable scraps
Plants
Hair
Sawdust
Eggshells, clean
Pet fur
Shredded newspaper
Wood ashes
Manure (from cows, horses, sheep, pigs, and chickens)

14

Fun Fact:
Keep your eyes open for the Kentucky state butterfly, the viceroy. They are very similar to the monarch in color and markings. They hide around willow trees, even using the leaves as little blankets.

Plants need water.

Plants drink water through their roots. Seeds need water to **germinate** and stay alive. Check plants every day to make sure your soil does not dry out. Plants enjoy a gentle rain or sprinkle of water. A hard rain or spray will wash away the seeds and damage the plant.

Most plants need about 1 inch of water a week. But...too much water can make plants sick.

Weeding is a very important part of gardening.

All gardens tend to attract **weeds**. If you allow weeds to take over your garden, your plants will not have "elbow room." Weeds will hog the soil, food, moisture and sun. Weeds need to be pulled as soon as they are spotted.

In order to tell which are weeds it is best to use a marker. Markers can be store-bought, or you can make your own from recycled popsicle sticks.

Some plants need mulch.

Mulching is a great way to conserve water and decrease weeds.

Mulch can be store-bought, or you can gather your own by using chopped leaves, straw, or dried grass. It is best to mulch 2 to 3 inches thick, but mulch should never touch the plant. Too much mulch can suffocate a plant.

The **life cycle** of a plant starts with a seed. As a small root grows down into the soil, a stem grows up toward the surface of the soil. Next, a stem will break through the soil and become a sprout.

Seed

Stem

Root

Sprout

When leaves begin to form on the plant stem, the seedling can make its own food.

The last stage of the life cycle
is when the seedling develops
into a plant similar to the plant
it came from. Plants can be
either an **annual**, **perennial**,
or **biennial**.

Annual: A plant that completes its
life cycle in one growing season.
It will grow, flower, set seed, and die.

Perennial: A plant that lives
year after year. It can grow,
flower, and set seed.

Biennial: A plant that needs
two growing seasons to
complete its life cycle. It
grows leaves one season.
Then it goes dormant, or
rests, over the winter. In
the spring, it will begin
to grow again and grow
flowers, set seed, and die.
The seed that is left behind
on the ground germinates,
and the cycle begins again.

Sowing Seeds

Easy seeds for children:

Sunflower
Zinnia
Marigolds
Lettuce
Carrots
Pumpkins
Beans

Seeds can be started in the garden or in any container with a hole in the bottom to drain water. Spacing of seeds and depth of planting are determined by the variety of plant you choose. Always read the directions on the seed packet for best results. After planting, water seeds carefully as to not wash away the soil. Check the soil for moisture loss every day. Do not over-water.

Some seeds sprout quicker if they are soaked in water overnight prior to sowing. Once you sow your seeds and get them wet, you must keep the soil moist. Soil should never be allowed to dry out until the seeds sprout.

If you planted seeds in a container, place the container in a sunny window.

After the seedlings begin to grow, you will find that you will need to remove a few seedlings to allow room for the biggest and healthiest seedlings to thrive. It is best to snip the seedlings that you need to eliminate with small scissors and not pull them out. Pulling seedlings will disturb the soil around the seedlings you want to keep growing.

If you have extra seeds, save them in a closed container and keep them in a cool dry place.

After the seeds sprout, plants grow a little bit every day.

If you are growing a flower, the plant will grow a bud at the top of the stem, and this bud will open into a flower. The flower holds seeds inside for future plants.

If you grow plants in a container, as they grow you may need to transplant them to a larger container or the garden. It is best to transplant on a mild day that is not too sunny or too cold. Move containers outside gradually so the plants get used to being outside. This process is called **hardening-off**.

When the plants are ready for their new home, gently remove them from their container or existing home and transplant them to their new home. If the plant is already in the garden, it is best to moisten the soil and take an ample amount of soil along for the ride to make sure the roots are not disturbed too much.

Water the soil well to remove air pockets from the soil and keep an eye on it for a few days.Keep the soil moist until the plant looks happy.

Fun Facts:

In 1926 Kentucky named the goldenrod (Solidago) to be its state flower. Its golden plumes can be seen in September across the state. It was thought that masses of goldenrod in the field pointed the way to a hidden treasure.

Plant a vegetable garden.

Growing your own food can be the most rewarding venture in gardening. Depending on what you want to grow, here are a few tips to make it a successful vegetable garden.

1. Make sure all the tall plants will be in the back so they won't shade the shorter plants.

2. Always read the packet or container to know how far to space and how far the plants will spread as they grow.

3. Some vegetables such as tomatoes will need to be **staked** or supported as they grow.

4. Keep your garden weed-free.

5. Make sure vegetables are watered as the soil dries.

Grow a row of carrots.

You will need:

Packet of carrot seeds *(choose a small variety)*
Soil that is free of rocks and sticks *(Remember, carrots like to grow down.)*

- Sow carrot seeds directly into the soil.
- Water every day until they germinate. Be patient because carrot seeds are slow to germinate.
- As foliage appears, thin seedlings every 3 inches to avoid overcrowding.

Carrots will mature in about 60 days.

Fun Fact:
Each strawberry plant
should produce one quart
of strawberries.

Grow a Strawberry Patch.

You will need:

10 to 12 strawberry plants
Aged manure or compost
Straw for mulching

The patch needs to receive full sun and drain well. You must be patient because the first year is a foliage year. The strawberries will produce in the next year.

- Prepare the site by improving soil with compost or aged manure.
- Create rows about 12 inches apart.
- Plant your strawberries spacing them 12 inches apart.
- Don't bury the crown, or center of the plant, too deep.
- After plants are in place, take the straw and mulch between the plants and rows.
- Water each plant well.

During the first few months, you will need to pick the flowers off the plants to allow the roots to grow strong. You will find that by picking off the flowers this year, you will have an abundance of strawberries next year. It is also good for the plants if you remove the runners, or new side shoots, from the plant for the first few years.

When winter comes, cover the plants with straw for protection and when spring arrives, remove the straw.

After the first few years allow the runners to spread, which creates new plants, and then you can remove the old, tired plant.

Plant a tree.

Trees benefit you and your community in many ways. They add character to neighborhoods, cool our cities, provide a home for wildlife, and clean our air. Once trees are planted they need to be trimmed, or pruned, and maintained so they can live a long, healthy life.

1 Make sure there is enough room for your tree to grow.
2 Make sure that you don't plant where utilities are above or below the ground.
3 Dig a hole that is 3 times the width of the root ball and the same height as the root ball.
4 Fill hole with water to make sure the site drains properly. If it doesn't drain well, choose a new site.
5 Remove all strings, tags and wire from rootball.
6 Place the tree in the center of the hole.
7 Fill hole with soil, and water thoroughly to remove air pockets.
8 Create a saucer of mulch around tree trunk. Avoid touching tree with mulch.
9 Water weekly, and then as needed to keep soil cool and moist.

Fun Facts:

An acre of trees can remove about 13 tons of dust
and gases from the air every year.

One tree can absorb as much carbon
dioxide in a year as a car produces
while driving 26,000 miles.

In one year an average-size tree can
produce enough oxygen for a family of four.

Since 1976 the Kentucky state tree has been the
yellow poplar or tulip poplar (Liriodendron tulipifera).
A member of the Magnolia family, its blooms have
yellow-green petals and an orange inner covering.

← 3 times the width of the root ball →

Create a Secret Teepee

You will need:

6 to 12 bamboo poles that are 6 feet long
Heavy twine
Seeds (morning glory, moon vine, scarlet runner bean, Kentucky pole beans)
Straw

1 Sink bamboo poles in the soil five inches deep,
   creating a 4 to 6 foot circle. Space poles evenly,
   allowing for a doorway to your teepee.
2 Use the twine to secure the top of the teepee about
   one foot from the top.
3 Wrap the twine around and through each pole to
   form a secure web. Work from the base of
   the teepee to the top. Don't forget to leave
   the doorway free of twine.
4 Plant seeds all around the base, avoiding
   the doorway. Space seeds as directed
   on seed packet.
5 Lay straw on the inside of teepee.
6 As the vine grows, give it
   a hand by directing it
   through the twine webbing.
7 Water as needed.
8 Remove weeds.

Butterfly Garden

Create a home for butterflies. Many flowers are sweet-smelling and brightly-colored for the purpose of attracting butterflies. They sip flower nectar through their tongues like a straw. They lay eggs on plants. Butterflies enjoy shelter from the weather and water to drink.

There are good and bad creatures in the garden. Dragonflies, ladybugs, birds, snakes, lizards, spiders, and frogs eat bad garden creatures. It is always a good idea to identify the **pest** before you kill it. Always ask an adult to assist you in ridding the garden of bugs and rodents.

Earthworms loosen the soil, allowing roots to grow better. They leave poop in the soil that turns into nutrients.

Be careful not to kill bees. They are important to plants because they carry **pollen**, which is the yellow powder at the center of a flower. Pollen makes seeds for future plants.

During **pollination**, bees, hummingbirds, and butterflies collect pollen from the flowers. They fly from flower to flower leaving the yellow powder behind. The bees also take the pollen back to their hives to make honey.

Glossary

ANNUAL - A plant that germinates, grows, flowers, and produces seeds in one growing season.

BIENNIAL - A plant which completes its life cycle in two seasons. In the first year it produces leaves and in the second year it blooms.

BUD - Early stage of flower development.

COMPOST - An organic soil amendment created from the breakdown of organic matter.

FERTILIZER - A material added to soil to provide additional nutrients for plants.

GERMINATE - The sprouting of a seed.

HARDENING-OFF - The process of gradually adjusting plants to the outdoors.

LEAVES - The above portion of a plant that takes in air and uses light to make food.

LIFE CYCLE - Shows how a living thing grows, lives, and dies.

MANURE - Organic matter, excreted by animals, which is used as a soil amendment and fertilizer.

MULCH - Any loose material placed over the soil to control weeds and conserve soil moisture.

ORGANIC - Method of gardening without use of man-made products.

ORGANIC MATTER - Anything that contains carbon compounds that were formed by living organisms. Examples include lawn clippings, leaves, stems, branches, manure, insects, and earthworms.

PERENNIAL - A plant that dies down to the ground during winter and survives to grow again each spring.

PEST - Any insect or animal which is harmful to the health of plants or other animals.

PHOTOSYNTHESIS - The internal process by which a plant converts sunlight into growing energy.

POLLEN - The yellow dust produced by the anthers of a flower.

POLLINATION - The transfer of pollen from the stamen (male part of the flower) to the pistil (female part of the flower), which results in the formation of a seed.

ROOTS - The underground portion of a plant that anchors the plant and takes in water and minerals.

SEEDS - A product of the parent plant that grows into a new plant.

SEEDLING - A young plant grown from seed.

STAKE - To support a plant by tying it to a post.

STEM - The above-ground portion of a plant that holds up the plant.

THINNING - Removing excess seedlings, to allow plenty of room for the remaining plants to grow.

TREE - A woody plant with a distinct central trunk.

WEED - An uninvited plant that surfaces in gardens competing for food, water and light.